2018

Myrlie re... ...om public life to dedicate
her ti... ...egacy of her late
first... ...s of
202... ...sary of
Me... ...makes public
appearances.

JANUARY 21, 2013

Myrlie became the first woman and
layperson to say a prayer at a presidential
inauguration, following President Barack
Obama's reelection for a second term.

DECEMBER 14 & 15, 2012

At the age of seventy-nine, Myrlie was
invited to play Carnegie Hall by Pink Martini, a
jazz band known for playing political events.

SEPTEMBER 23, 2009

Myrlie received the National Freedom Award for
lifetime achievement by the National Civil Rights
Museum in Memphis, Tennessee.

JULY 15, 1998

Myrlie accepted the NAACP's highest
honor, the Spingarn Medal, for her
civil rights work. Coretta Scott King
presented her with the medal.

1996

Myrlie funded the Medgar Evers Institute with
donations from the film premiere of Hollywood
director Rob Reiner's *Ghosts of Mississippi*, a
movie about the 1994 trial that brought her family
justice for Medgar's murder.

FEBRUARY 18, 1995

Myrlie ran for the NAACP's chairperson seat and won. She became the
first woman to hold this seat position full-time. Days later, her second
husband, Walter Edward Williams, died of cancer. Myrlie carries the title
of chair emeritus for serving the organization with distinction.

"I believe we have a reason for being." —Myrlie Evers-Williams

Use your voice to change the world. —N. S. A.
For Lavanda —L. L.

AUTHOR'S ACKNOWLEDGMENTS

Myrlie Evers-Williams; Reena Evers-Everette; Linda C. Giffin; Hilda Gudino; Ida Mercado-Ramirez;
Jerry Mitchell and the Mississippi Center for Investigative Reporting (MCIR);
India Artis, the NAACP, and *The Crisis* magazine; Stacey Chandler, Maryrose Grossman,
and the John F. Kennedy Presidential Library and Museum.

A very special thank-you to all of my critique partners: The OGs, Swapsters, WB Friends,
and Truckee Troop. And my wonderful agent, Ammi-Joan Paquette.

PHILOMEL
An imprint of Penguin Random House LLC
1745 Broadway, New York, New York 10019

First published in the United States of America by Philomel,
an imprint of Penguin Random House LLC, 2024

Visit us online at PenguinRandomHouse.com.

Library of Congress Cataloging-in-Publication Data is available.

ISBN 9780593525913

1 3 5 7 9 10 8 6 4 2

Manufactured in China

TOPL

Edited by Jill Santopolo
Design by Lucia Baez · Text set in Songti SC

The art for this book was created with acrylic paint, cut paper, tissue paper, and colored pencil on an illustration board.

A VOICE OF HOPE
THE MYRLIE EVERS-WILLIAMS STORY

Written by **NADIA SALOMON**   Illustrated by **LONDON LADD**

PHILOMEL

MYRLIE EVERS-WILLIAMS stood before the
nation on a chilly January day . . .

Her voice—strong
yet gentle.
Soft
yet powerful.
Soaring—like a song spreading hope.

But Myrlie's voice didn't start out that way.

Myrlie Louise Beasley was born on a green and sunny
St. Patrick's Day in Vicksburg, Mississippi.
But she entered an unkind world . . .

Myrlie grew up in a place where hate ran as deep as the Mississippi
and Yazoo rivers.
A place where white people did not see Black people as equal.

A place where brown skin made little girls like Myrlie a target.
And forced her to fight for her life.

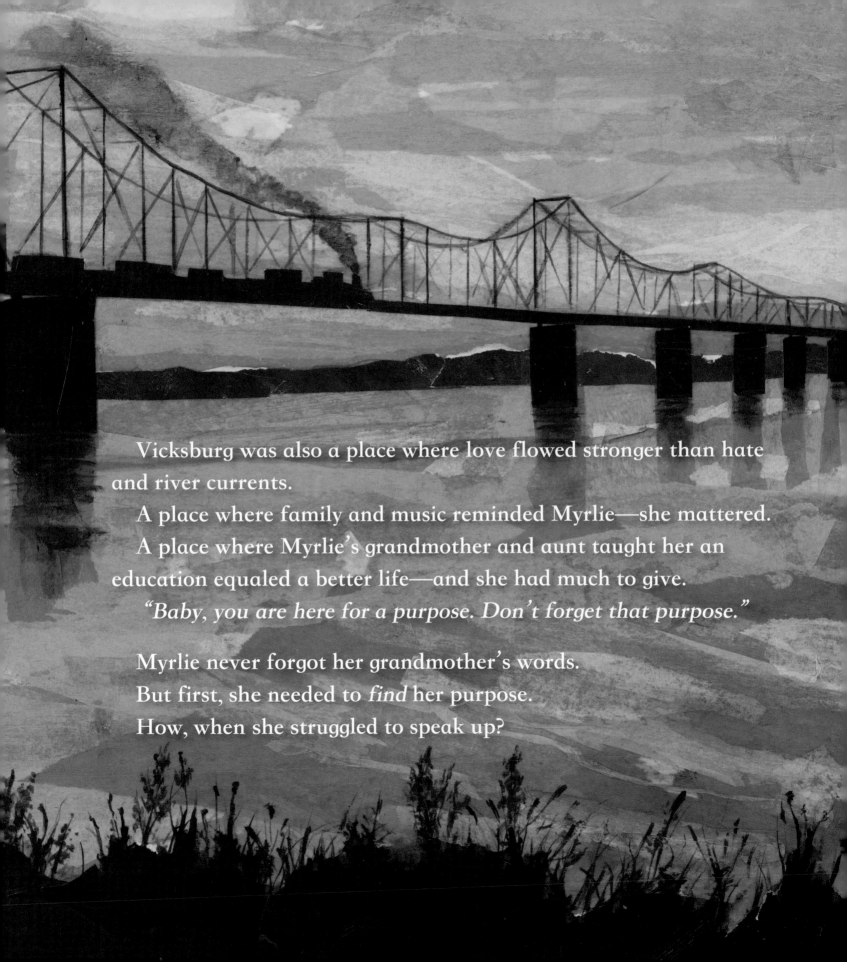

Vicksburg was also a place where love flowed stronger than hate and river currents.

A place where family and music reminded Myrlie—she mattered.

A place where Myrlie's grandmother and aunt taught her an education equaled a better life—and she had much to give.

"Baby, you are here for a purpose. Don't forget that purpose."

Myrlie never forgot her grandmother's words.

But first, she needed to *find* her purpose.

How, when she struggled to speak up?

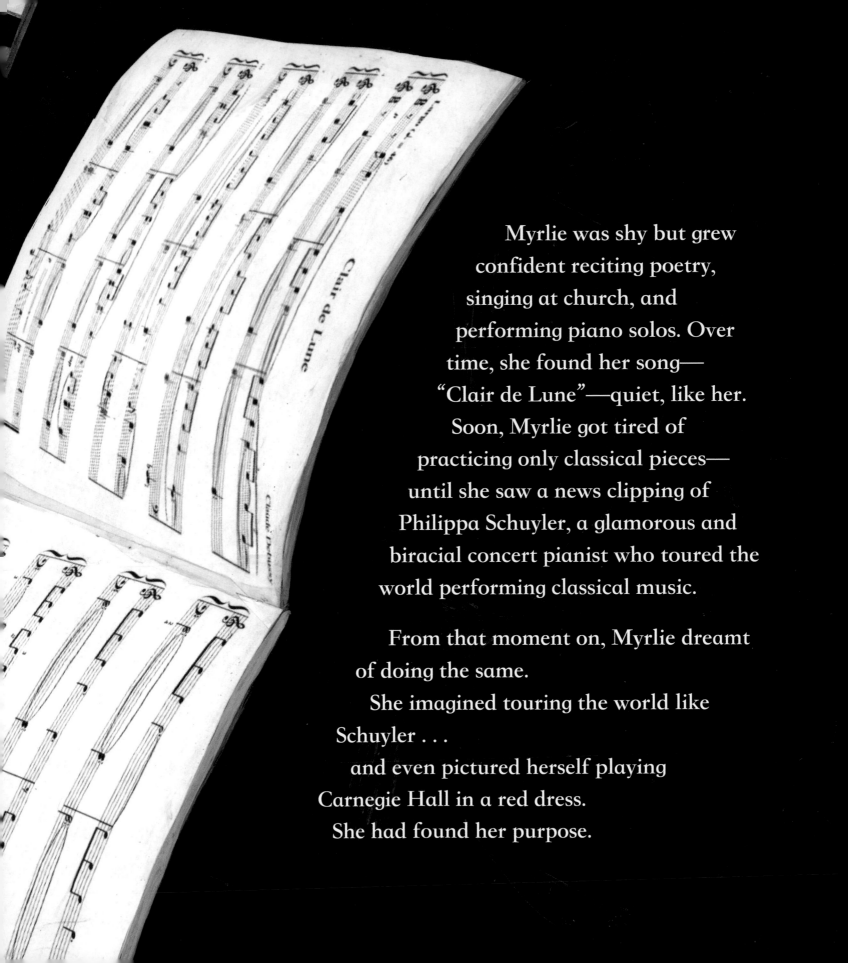

Myrlie was shy but grew confident reciting poetry, singing at church, and performing piano solos. Over time, she found her song—"Clair de Lune"—quiet, like her. Soon, Myrlie got tired of practicing only classical pieces—until she saw a news clipping of Philippa Schuyler, a glamorous and biracial concert pianist who toured the world performing classical music.

From that moment on, Myrlie dreamt of doing the same.
She imagined touring the world like Schuyler . . .
and even pictured herself playing Carnegie Hall in a red dress.
She had found her purpose.

"Baby, don't get your hopes up too high or you may be disappointed," her grandmother said.

Myrlie's heart sank.

She knew what her grandmother meant; she looked nothing like Schuyler.

Her skin was too brown. Her hair was too curly. And she was too poor.

Myrlie's dream and purpose suddenly felt out of reach.

But hope kept Myrlie strong against doubt. Hope also gave her
strength against hate—even when hate *hurt*.

Like when white people told Myrlie she was "nothing."

When she couldn't enter her city's public library.

When neighborhood bullies spat and hurled rocks at her on the
way to school.

And when neither silence nor sidestepping those
bullies made a difference, Myrlie's anger swelled to
a crescendo.

Instead of raising her soft voice
to say "Stop," she rallied her
friends.

Together, they raised
their fists and fought
back.

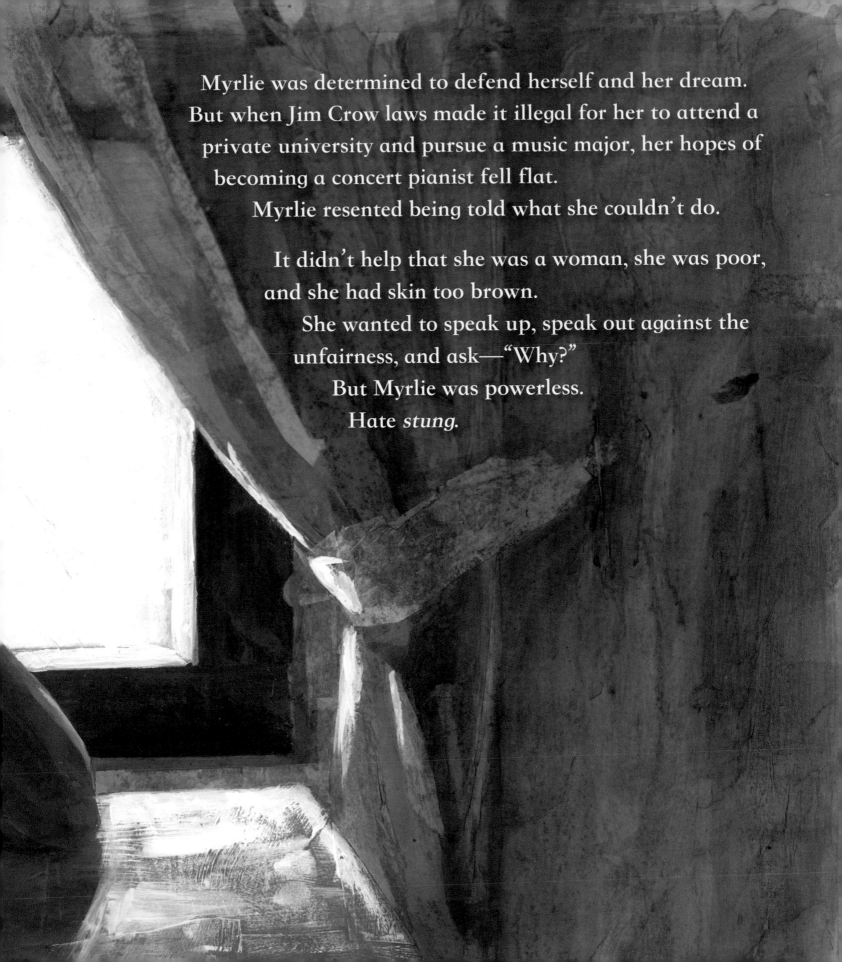

Myrlie was determined to defend herself and her dream.
But when Jim Crow laws made it illegal for her to attend a
private university and pursue a music major, her hopes of
becoming a concert pianist fell flat.
Myrlie resented being told what she couldn't do.

It didn't help that she was a woman, she was poor,
and she had skin too brown.
She wanted to speak up, speak out against the
unfairness, and ask—"Why?"
But Myrlie was powerless.
Hate *stung*.

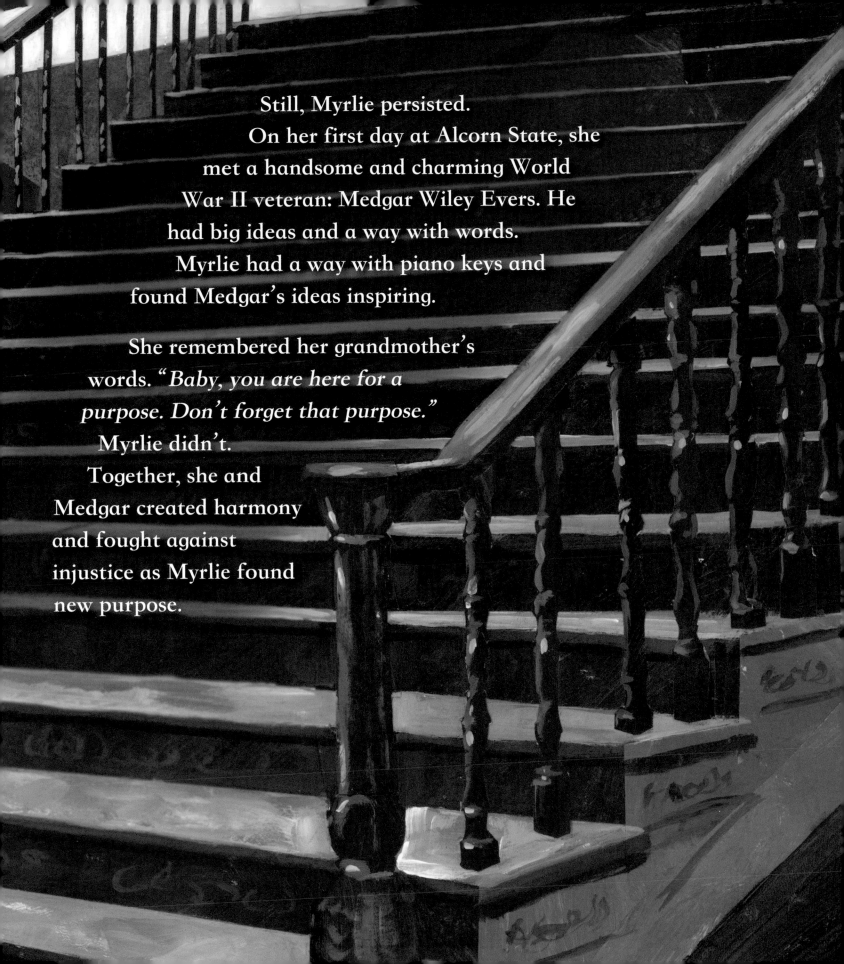

Still, Myrlie persisted.
On her first day at Alcorn State, she
met a handsome and charming World
War II veteran: Medgar Wiley Evers. He
had big ideas and a way with words.
Myrlie had a way with piano keys and
found Medgar's ideas inspiring.

She remembered her grandmother's
words. *"Baby, you are here for a
purpose. Don't forget that purpose."*
Myrlie didn't.
Together, she and
Medgar created harmony
and fought against
injustice as Myrlie found
new purpose.

With the world around her spinning out of tune, Myrlie's dream of performing at Carnegie Hall faded.

But she kept her passion for music close and continued to play piano at home—as a wife and mother.

Day by day, her quiet voice grew stronger.

For years Myrlie juggled family duties and civil rights work. The work was exhausting and dangerous.

Alongside Medgar, Myrlie marched against racism—even when her feet hurt.

She picketed for the right to vote—even when her warrior
spirit was tired.
She orchestrated sit-ins—even when her family faced terror.
Hate threatened.

One night, hours following President John F. Kennedy's address for unity, more division came instead.

As Medgar walked from his car to his doorway—a shot rang out.

Hate killed.

Myrlie's raging voice pierced the dark—ENOUGH!

While the gospel hymn "We Shall Overcome" echoed around Myrlie,
she held on to a folded flag.

Medgar was now a hero. And Myrlie felt seen.

Human.

Valued.

Nearly twenty-five thousand people, Black and white, lined the streets to
mourn with her.

Through this outpouring of support following Medgar's funeral, Myrlie
realized she had a legacy to uphold. This made her purpose stronger than
ever, and she picked up where Medgar left off. Myrlie stopped playing piano
to focus on her children, her education, and the battle for civil rights. And she
pushed for justice in honor of Medgar.

After thirty-one long years . . .
a guilty verdict was finally dealt to Medgar's killer.

Through justice, at long last, Myrlie laid Medgar's memory to rest.

The conviction was bittersweet, and so was Myrlie's victory one year later when she became the first woman to chair the NAACP on a full-time basis.

In time, the music Myrlie had lost found its way back into her heart.
She returned to playing piano—and her dream to play Carnegie Hall.

Then in December 2012, a friend invited
Myrlie to do just that.
   One wintry night, all eyes fixed on
Myrlie—concert pianist.
   She performed her defining song—
"Clair de Lune"—in a beautiful red dress.

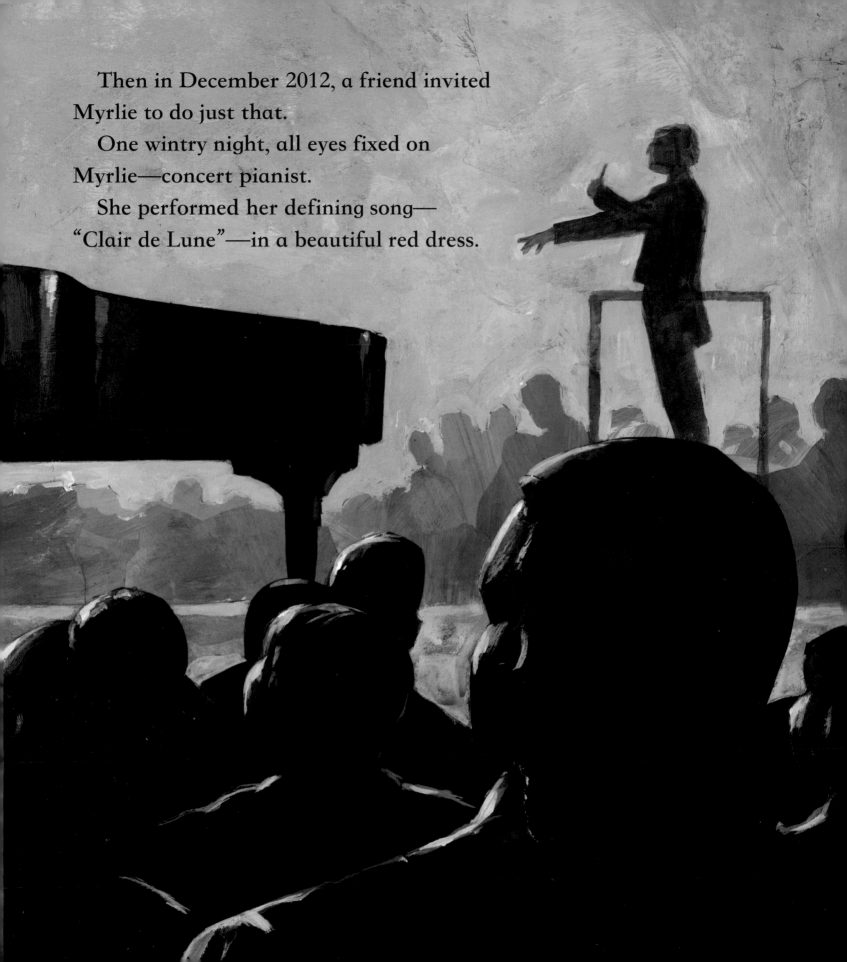

A month later, following the reelection of President Barack Obama, the nation's eyes focused on Myrlie again as she became the first non-clergyperson to say a prayer at a presidential inauguration.

Throughout her life, Myrlie had pushed against racism. She gave much of herself to impact change—and she never forgot her grandmother's words.

On that chilly January day, on the steps of the Capitol, Myrlie reminded the world that even a quiet voice can grow powerful.

Her voice rang out like a symphony—

Strong. Soft. Soaring.

And her words echoed hope.